Britain in World War Two
Resource Book

Contents

The Outbreak of War	2
War is Declared	2
A National Emergency	4
Families	6
The Blackout	7
Gas Masks	8
Fighting the War	10
Winston Churchill	10
Dunkirk	12
The Battle of Britain	14
The War at Home	18
Rationing	18
Government Posters	20
The Wireless	22
Newsreels	25
G.I.s	26
Towards Peace	28
D-Day	28
The End of the War	30
Memorabilia	32

The Outbreak of War

War is Declared

On September 3rd 1939, the Prime Minister used the radio to announce that Britain and France were at war with Germany. It was a shock, but not a surprise.

From April, all men aged between twenty-one and twenty-two had been 'called up'. They had been **conscripted**. In the summer they did their training and by September 3rd, they were ready to sail to Europe.

The war would be fought in the air as well as on land and sea. Many people could be hurt or killed.

The newsboy has written the word 'official' because the country had been expecting this to happen all that year.

Conscripted

Men had to join the army, whether they wanted to or not.

The Outbreak of War

By July, the Women's Land Army were waiting to be sent to farms to help produce more food. In wartime, supplies from overseas are often cut off.

Here they are marching in front of the King and Queen.

Do you think the sandbags would have saved this building?

These sandbags have been put up round a hospital. If there was a bomb attack, the doctors and nurses hoped that the sandbags would muffle the sound. They might help protect the windows and even save the walls of the building if the bombs were not too near.

When children went back to school, some of the **shelters** had already been built.

◆ What are the shelters like?

◆ What are the children doing?

◆ Do they look scared?

Shelter
A safe place, usually underground, to go to if bombs began to fall.

A National Emergency

On September 2nd 1939 both Houses of Parliament met to prepare for an emergency. Perhaps they drew up a list of questions like this:

> Are there enough uniforms for them to wear, food for them to eat, guns and weapons for them to use?

> Are there enough soldiers, sailors and airmen to fight a war?

> Who will be in command of each section of the forces (the Army, the Navy and the Air Force)?

> Are there enough trains, tanks, ships and aircraft to move the troops to where they will be needed?

> Where will the fighting take place?

> Are there enough doctors, nurses, ambulances, bandages and drugs to look after the injured?

Troops

Soldiers, sailors and airmen fighting the war.

The Outbreak of War

They had to think about the people at home as well:

What if the Germans dropped poisonous gas, which had been used in the First World War?

What would stop German aircraft seeing buildings and streets from the air?

What would happen if German bombs dropped on British civilians?

Food and clothes would be in short supply when all the factories started to make things for the war. How should they be shared out fairly?

What sort of shelters should be built and where?

How could the government keep everyone informed about what was going on?

How would the war be paid for?

Who would do the jobs the men in the forces left behind?

How many children should be evacuated?

Civilians
People not in the army, navy or air force.

Evacuate

GOVERNMENT EVACUATION SCHEME
CITY OF GLASGOW
NAME
ADDRESS
DATE OF BIRTH OF CHILD
SCHOOL ATTENDED

To send children from places which were likely to be bombed to places where they would be safe.

The Outbreak of War

Families

This picture shows two points of view about the beginning of the war. It shows that the war was not just about the people who went to fight but about the ones who were left behind at home as well.

The soldier was going to join the war. Can you see his uniform and the bag on his back? He had things for a journey in it. He did not know when he would see the boy again.

On September 1st 1939 it became law for all men between the ages of eighteen and forty-one to **join up**. The evacuation of children began on September 1st.

This boy is being evacuated

- Look at the label on his coat.
- Look at the box over his shoulder. His gasmask is inside.
- What do you think was in the parcel in his right hand?
- Do you think the boy understands what is happening?
- What do you think they are saying to each other?
- Why did someone decide to take the photograph?

Join up
To become a soldier, sailor or airman.

The Outbreak of War

The Blackout

Another new law was the use of the 'blackout' after dark. This was to stop people in aeroplanes from seeing streets, homes and cities on the ground.

What did you have to carry if you wanted to be seen at night?

What does this poster tell us about the trains in the blackout?

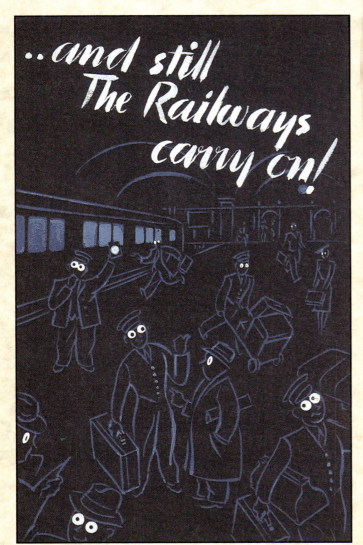

BLACKOUT RULES

No street lights. Traffic lights, car lights, bicycle lights and torches to have a black hood.

Blinds on the windows of buses and trains.

Carry a white handkerchief in the street if you want other people to see you.

Cover all windows at home with black curtains, blinds or brown paper.

Make sure that no light shows outside.

The blackout made it very difficult for people to get about safely. Road accidents increased. A government information leaflet said,

> "When you first come out into the blackout, stand still for a minute and get your eyes used to the darkness."

How useful do you think this advice was, particularly if you were an elderly person?

The Outbreak of War

Gas Masks

From September 3rd 1939 everyone had to carry their gas mask wherever they went. This was in case bombs of poisonous gas were dropped by the enemy. The gas mask had a pan inside which filtered any poison out of the air before it could be breathed in.

Here is a poster issued by a new government department, the Department of Home Security.

♦ Do you think it frightened people or made them feel safer? Remember, Hitler was the German leader.

Young children were given a gas mask which was supposed to look like Mickey Mouse. It was red and blue and had a long flap on the front. It looked like this to make little children laugh instead of feeling frightened. The gas mask is made of thin rubber. It fitted tightly round the face.

♦ Do you think it looks funny or frightening?
♦ What do you think it felt like and smelt like when it was put on?

The Outbreak of War

Children learnt how to put their gas masks on and take them off at school. Sometimes they had to wear them during lessons, so that they would get used to them.

These children in Huddersfield had to do P.E. wearing gas masks.

The children had to learn to breathe wearing a gas mask. Here is what one girl remembers,

> "I remember when the gas masks were first issued at school. Some very rude raspberry noises were made. One had to breathe out quite strongly in order to force out the air, whereupon it gave out a rather rude raspberry kind of noise. Of course we children were delighted in blowing raspberries all over class."

But gas masks were never needed for a real gas attack as no poisonous gas was ever dropped.

♦ Do you think the government were sensible or foolish to issue everyone with one?

Fighting the War

Winston Churchill

In May 1940, Mr Chamberlain the Prime Minister resigned. Winston Churchill was asked to take his place and lead a 'coalition' government. This was for the sake of national unity. It meant there would only be one side in Parliament, instead of two or three different parties, and that they would all support Mr Churchill. He was invited to be Minister for Defence as well as Prime Minister.

This poster was placed all over Britain. Find:
- Churchill.
- planes.
- tanks.

Fighting the War

The map shows you why Britain needed a strong government. The Germans were winning the war in Europe. Why do you think the British government thought this was a very serious situation? Remember that thousands of British soldiers had been sent to France only six months earlier.

Where do you think Hitler planned to attack next?

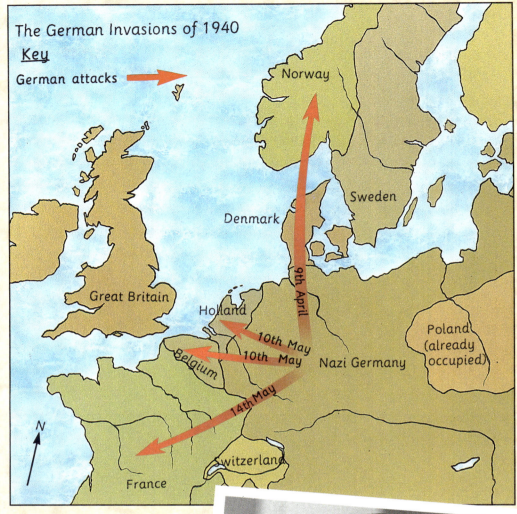

In Parliament Mr Churchill made the first of his war speeches. He wanted to make people believe that he would make a tremendous effort to lead the country in what he called it's 'hour of need'. He promised that he would give his 'blood, toil, tears and sweat'. Words like these encouraged Members of Parliament and other people, when they heard the speech read out on the wireless, to make a great effort too.

That night the government rushed a new law through Parliament. It was called the Emergency Powers Act which said that the Minister of Labour, Mr Ernest Bevin, could take control of everything in the country, including coal mines, farms, factories, and buildings, that were needed for the war effort.

Here is a picture of Ernest Bevin the Minister of Labour. He had an important job in the war.

Fighting the War

Dunkirk

The situation in France was very bad for British and French soldiers.

The British army had nowhere to go except into a small area of northern France. They arrived exhausted, lay down on the beach and looked across the English Channel. They hoped someone would come and rescue them as they could hear the German army coming closer.

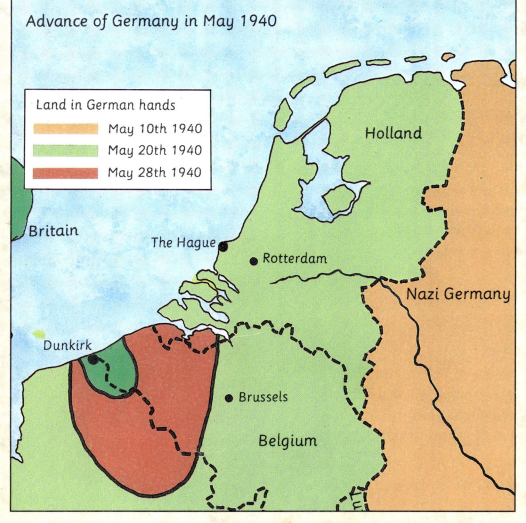

Look at the map. It shows the parts of Europe controlled by the German army in May 1940. Find:

- Luxembourg.
- Germany.
- Belgium.
- Holland.
- France.
- Britain.

Fighting the War

It was time for the navy to play an important part in the war. An emergency meeting was called on May 20th 1940 to organise what they called Operation Dynamo. They would try to evacuate all the British troops from the beaches. But how could it be done?

The navy warships were too big to get up to the beaches, so an appeal was put out over the radio on the 9 o'clock News. The navy asked for anyone who had a small boat such as a fishing boat or a boat they used for their holidays to come forward. If the boat was strong enough to cross the English Channel it was needed, with the owner and crew, to take soldiers from the beaches to the big warships.

Between May 27th and June 4th 1940, 338,226 people were rescued with the help of these little boats and brought back to Britain.

Unfortunately, not everyone arrived home alive. If you visit northern France today you can see the graves of some of those who did not return.

In the painting above find:

- soldiers getting into boats.
- the small boats.
- the big warships.
- planes.
- smoke from bombs.

This is what some of the graves looked like. The stone would have been put up after the war.

Fighting the War

The Battle of Britain

Most people think that the evacuation of the army from Dunkirk was a victory. Other people think it was a terrible defeat. The German army had taken over nearly the whole of Europe. They moved into Paris and in June 1940 they occupied part of Britain, the Channel Islands.

Mr Churchill said,

> "The Battle of France is over. I expect that the Battle of Britain is about to begin."

The attack came from the sky. Many people fought in the Battle of Britain.

These women used radar to find the German planes as they approached the south coast of Britain.

They telephoned these pilots from the Royal Air Force (RAF) who ran to get into their Spitfires to fight the German Air Force, called the Luftwaffe.

Spitfire
A fighter plane used by the Royal Air Force.

Blitz
From a German word. A sudden attack from the air.

Fighting the War

But the Battle of Britain wasn't just fought in the air. Down on the ground thousands of ordinary people were bombed. Every night in most of the big cities like Hull, Bristol, Southampton, Glasgow, Belfast and London, the sirens sounded to warn people that an air raid was on the way.

Some people had shelters in their back garden. They only measured just over 2 metres by 1.5 metres.

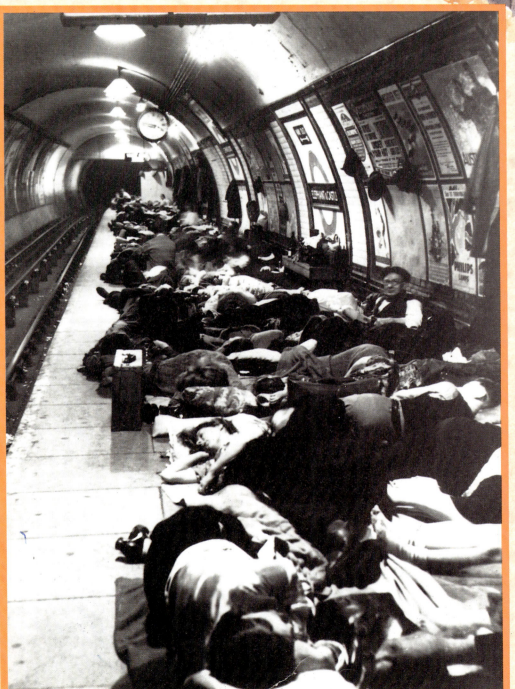

♦ How do you think a family of five fitted the beds in?

♦ What else do you think they took into the shelter with them?

Many families did not have a shelter of their own. They took their camp beds and blankets to the Underground stations.

♦ Can you see the man who is awake?

♦ How well do you think they could sleep in there?

Fighting the War

The Germans wanted to do more than just frighten people. They wanted to destroy factories, docks, airfields and railway lines all over Britain. They used photographs taken from the air to find out where these were. Why do you think that destroying these places would help them to win the war?

This map shows where some of the worst raids were and the reason for them. However, many smaller places all over Britain were targets too. Find out if your town was bombed in the war and what the target was.

factories

shipyard

tank parts

steelworks

centre of government

docks

Royal Navy base

aircraft factory

NORTH SEA

Glasgow

Belfast

Liverpool • Manchester

Hull

Sheffield

Birmingham

Coventry

Cardiff

Bristol

London

Southampton

Portsmouth

N

ENGLISH CHANNEL

Fighting the War

Many ordinary people were very brave during the blitz. In shelters they sang to keep their spirits up. Someone wrote this message on a pub wall in the East End of London.

Men and women of all ages volunteered to do 'war work'. They were issued with helmets, called 'tin hats', protective uniforms, stirrup pumps and buckets for water. Their jobs were to help people after an air raid. They were air raid wardens, first aid workers, firewatchers or in the Home Guard.

Between September 1940 and May 1941 about 43,000 civilians were killed in the war.

What was the cartoonist trying to say?

Keep smiling – He may get us up but he'll never get us down!

Here is one ARP warden rescuing a child from a house where a bomb has fallen. She was one of the lucky ones.

ARP
Air Raid Precautions.

The War at Home

Rationing

Everyone became involved in fighting the Second World War, some with weapons in the army, navy or air force; others in their own home towns.

Mothers had a particularly important part to play. This was because food was rationed. On average each person had:

One shilling, two pence (1s.2d) worth of meat

One ounce of cheese

Four ounces of bacon or ham

Two ounces of tea

Eight ounces of sugar

Eight ounces of butter or fat

Note:
1 ounce = 25 grams.
1s 2d = 7p. This bought 2 ounces of corned beef.

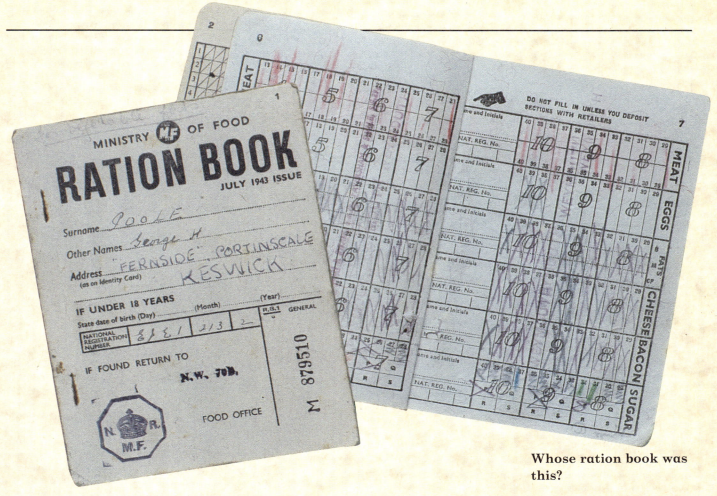

Whose ration book was this?

Fruit and vegetables were not on ration, but some were in short supply as food from the farms had to go to feed those in uniform.

The government told people to 'Dig for Victory' and grow as much of their own food as they could.

Some clothing factories were busy making uniforms for the forces. Clothes were rationed, so it was impossible to buy many new ones.

What did women have to do if they wanted new clothes for themselves and their families?

Government Posters

The Government wanted everyone to contribute to the war effort. They published posters and sent many information leaflets through everyone's letter box. They also thought up some short slogans or catchphrases to put on the posters.

Look at these two posters:

Trains were needed to move soldiers and airmen from their camps to where they were needed. The government did not want civilians taking up seats on the trains.

What did people have to think about before making any journeys?

Many men who were factory workers had been conscripted so thousands of women were needed to work instead. Everything made in the factories was needed for the war. Women worked making planes, shells and other ammunition, uniforms, parachutes, tanks, warships, submarines and medical supplies like bandages.

This poster encouraged women to go to work in the factories.

The War at Home

In 1941 all unmarried women between the ages of twenty and thirty were conscripted.

They could choose to work either in a factory, on the land or in some of the women's sections of the army, navy or air force. These were called the auxiliary servies and supported the troops.

Women were not allowed to go to the front where the actual fighting was going on, although many wanted to. Do you think this was right?

There were plenty of other things for women to do. Married women were not conscripted, but they could volunteer if they wanted to. Many preferred to organise their war effort themselves.

Others joined the WVS (Women's Voluntary Service). They helped distribute clothes, food and furniture to people who had been bombed out.

What do you think this poster is trying to get people to do?

These women met every week to knit socks, jumpers, hats and scarves for people in the war.

The War at Home

The Wireless

Did you notice that the women in the knitting party were listening to the radio? This was called 'the wireless' in the Second World War and it was very important in people's lives.

At 9 o'clock at night, all over Britain, people listened to the News. The first thing they heard was the sound of Big Ben. Then the newscaster would say his name (only men read the News in those days). Listeners recognised these voices. They felt secure when they heard them. It told them that the Germans had not invaded. If they had, they would have taken over the BBC.

Mr Churchill made many stirring speeches on the radio during the war years. He did this both to encourage ordinary people to have faith in the government and to keep up their support of the war effort.

This picture was taken in 1940.
- What is the family listening for?
- What do you think the newsreader is saying?

The War at Home

He also knew that the broadcasts could be heard in Germany. He wanted Hitler to known that Britain would never give up. In one of his most famous speeches he said,

"We will never surrender.".

The wireless was also important for two other things. It gave out information, particularly hints about keeping healthy, growing vegetables and making the most of the rations.

There was even a Radio Doctor. He told people about the importance of diet and vitamins and how to treat themselves for minor illnesses like colds.

Recipes were given out on the radio to help cooks vary the meals, even though food was rationed. One of them for a vegetable pie. It was called Woolton Pie after the Minister of Food. Remember, vegetables were not rationed.

◆ What does the 'Kitchen Front' remind you of?

The wireless also played music and comedy to help keep people's minds off the war. Every morning 'Music While You Work' was played. It was put on in factories and hospitals as well as in homes.

Vera Lynn, a singer of the time was also called the 'Forces Sweetheart'. The songs she sang were sentimental and patriotic such as; 'We'll meet again' and 'The White Cliffs of Dover', but they cheered people up.

Here she is singing to some of those who are on active service.

> **On active service**
> Fighting in the war.

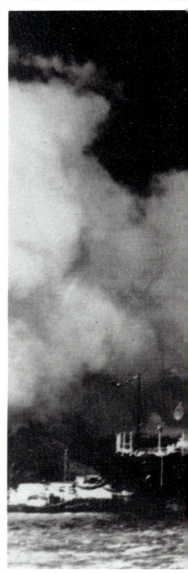

Another programme which went out every week was ITMA. These letters stood for 'It's That Man Again'. The comedian who made everyone laugh was Tommy Handley.

There were a lot of catchphrases in the programmes like 'After you Cecil' which people used to repeat.

The War at Home

Newsreels

No one had television in the Second World War, but sometimes they went to the cinema. There they could see the newsreel of Pathé Pictorial. This often showed films of what was going on outside Britain and reminded people that others in Europe were worse off than themselves.

A British army, with troops from all over the Commonwealth was fighting the Germans in North Africa.

Germany had invaded Greece and Russia. Many thousands of people there were sent to prison camps.

In December 1941 there came a turning point in the war. The Japanese, who were on the side of the Germans, bombed American ships at a place called Pearl Harbor

America came into the war on the side of the **allies**.

> **Allies**
> Friends. In the Second World War Britain, France, Russia and the USA were all allies. Soldiers from the British Commonwealth were part of the British army.

Here is a news photograph taken at the time of the Pearl Harbor bombing.

The War at Home

G.I.s

In January 1942, the first American soldiers arrived in Britain. Most British people had never met an American before, but they had seen American films. They thought that all the soldiers would look and behave like filmstars.

The British called them G.I.s because all their packs and equipment was labelled 'G.I. Government Issue'. They were also called 'Yanks'. They had more money than the British and were well known for their generosity.

What presents do you think the G.I.s are giving the children?

The War at Home

They also introduced some new words to the British. Some of the things they gave away were:

Gum – Chewing gum

Candy – Sweets and chocolate

Nylons – Fine stockings for women

The American soldiers were given a booklet about the British when they landed.

Here is part of what it said:

Do you think this information influenced the Americans when they met British civilians?

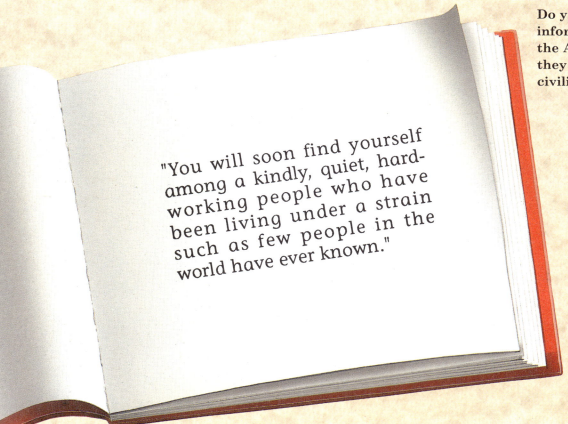

"You will soon find yourself among a kindly, quiet, hard-working people who have been living under a strain such as few people in the world have ever known."

The Americans were popular with many young women in Britain. Some of them married G.I.s and, after the war, went to America to live.

The American President was Mr Roosevelt. With the rest of the allies, he helped plan the next and final stage in the war.

Towards Peace

D-Day

Most people liked to think that the South Downs in Kent looked like this but in April and May 1944 Mr Churchill wrote in his diary that southern England was like a 'vast military camp'.

Visitors to any of the seaside towns in Sussex or Hampshire, were forbidden in case anyone noticed the secret army camps, the tanks, lorries guns and ships that were being hidden nearby for an important attack on the Germans in France.

What idea does this poster give about that part of Sussex? Find:

- the man.
- his dog.
- the empty countryside.

Towards Peace

Ever since their defeat at Dunkirk, the British hoped to return with an army to France, even though the war had spread from Europe to North Africa, Japan and Burma.

By 1944, the Germans were much weaker and had suffered many defeats in Italy and North Africa.

The allies, under the command of the American General Eisenhower, knew it was time to plan a secret landing in France.

June 6th 1944 was a terrible day for weather. High seas made crossing the English Channel very difficult, but the plan, called Operation Overlord, went ahead. Between midnight and dawn the first British and Canadian troops landed on the Normandy beaches. Allied airmen were dropped into France by parachute.

This photograph was taken some time during the day.

- Look at the equipment the soldiers have to carry on their backs.
- What do you think they felt like?

Remember they have just come off a ship after crossing a rough sea and that there was a lot of noise from aircraft in the sky.

Towards Peace

This medal was given to everyone who fought in the war.

The End of the War

The end of the war came in May 1945 after almost a year of heavy fighting. Many men, women and children were killed or injured. The RAF had heavily bombed German cities.

Hitler killed himself as the allies marched towards Berlin.

On **VE Day** in London Mr Churchill put on his best clothes. He went to the House of Commons. Then he spoke to the country on the radio and then he went on to the balcony at Buckingham Palace with the King and Queen.

All over Britain, people decided it was time to have some fun. They danced in the street, held parties and got ready to welcome the soldiers home.

Three months later on, it was **VJ Day** and peace was signed with the Japanese too.

Find:
- the King.
- Churchill.
- our Queen, Elizabeth.

VE Day
Victory in Europe Day.

VJ Day
Victory over Japan Day.

Towards Peace

Look at this family in Kilburn with Private Bill Martin. His mother and four sisters had not seen him for nearly four years. The children in the family cannot really remember him at all. He has been travelling for a long time, carrying all his belongings in one kitbag.

- Can you see his kitbag?
- Can you see his family?

How do you think they feel?

All over Britain people celebrated. Many can still remember the day of the street party. Although food was still rationed, everyone living in this street in Huddersfield contributed to a Victory Cake.

This is how one woman remembered the time,

> "Everybody brought their table out and the chairs and put them together. The piano was going. Oh! it was lovely.".

Towards Peace

Memorabilia

Many people still have reminders at home of the part they played in the Second World War and the sacrifices that were made. Every schoolchild had a message from the King.

How do you think the children of the time felt to be given such a message?

Every year on November 11th, people wear red poppies to remind them of all those who died in the two World Wars.

Why do you think it is important to do this?

8th June, 1946

To-day, as we celebrate victory, I send this personal message to you and all other boys and girls at school. For you have shared in the hardships and dangers of a total war and you have shared no less in the triumph of the Allied Nations.

I know you will always feel proud to belong to a country which was capable of such supreme effort; proud, too, of parents and elder brothers and sisters who by their courage, endurance and enterprise brought victory. May these qualities be yours as you grow up and join in the common effort to establish among the nations of the world unity and peace.

George R.I.